Most Amazing Bridges

Suzanne Harper

Series Editor
Jeffrey D. Wilhelm

Much thought, debate, and research went into choosing and ranking the 10 items in each book in this series. We realize that everyone has his or her own opinion of what is most significant, revolutionary, amazing, deadly, and so on. As you read, you may agree with our choices, or you may be surprised — and that's the way it should be!

an imprint of

SCHOLASTIC

www.scholastic.com/librarypublishing

A Rubicon book published in association with Scholastic Inc.

Rubicon © 2007 Rubicon Publishing Inc.
www.rubiconpublishing.com

All rights reserved. No part of this publication may be reproduced, stored in a database or retrieval system, distributed, or transmitted in any form or by any means, electronic, mechanical, photocopying, recording, or otherwise, without the prior written permission of Rubicon Publishing Inc.

 is a trademark of The 10 Books

SCHOLASTIC and associated logos and designs are trademarks and/or registered trademarks of Scholastic Inc.

Associate Publishers: Kim Koh, Miriam Bardswich
Project Editor: Amy Land
Editor: Dona Foucault
Creative Director: Jennifer Drew
Project Manager/Designer: Jeanette MacLean
Graphic Designer: Julie Whatman

The publisher gratefully acknowledges the following for permission to reprint copyrighted material in this book.

Every reasonable effort has been made to trace the owners of copyrighted material and to make due acknowledgment. Any errors or omissions drawn to our attention will be gladly rectified in future editions.

Cover: Golden Gate Bridge–Getty Images/Photographer's Choice/Mitchell Funk

Library and Archives Canada Cataloguing in Publication

Harper, Suzanne
    The 10 most amazing bridges / Suzanne Harper.

Includes index.
ISBN 978-1-55448-470-6

    1. Readers (Elementary) 2. Readers—Bridges. I. Title. II. Title: Ten most amazing bridges.

PE1117.H389 2007   428.6   C2007-900552-7

1 2 3 4 5 6 7 8 9 10   10   16 15 14 13 12 11 10 09 08 07

Printed in Singapore

Contents

Introduction:
Now We're Getting Somewhere! 4

Rainbow Bridge 6
How can a bridge that you can't even drive or walk across be amazing? Read this chapter to find out.

Monet's Bridge 10
What's so hot about a green, wooden footbridge? This one is featured in some of the world's most loved art.

Kawarau Bridge 14
The gold miners who used this bridge in the 1880s probably never imagined that 100 years later people would line up to bungee jump off it.

Quebec Bridge 18
Although it holds the record as the longest cantilevered bridge in the world, this bridge has a dark past.

Cendere Bridge 22
The Romans built things to last — including bridges. After 1,800 years, this one's holding up just fine. In fact, it is still in use.

Lupu Bridge 26
With a main span of more than 1,800 feet, the Lupu is the longest arch bridge in the world.

Golden Gate Bridge 30
Only one engineer was willing to take a stab at building this bridge. Fog, high winds, and rains scared other engineers away.

London Bridge 34
The London Bridge has more lives than a cat. It has been built and torn down at least 10 times.

Akashi Kaikyo Bridge 38
This suspension bridge holds records as the tallest, longest, and most expensive to build.

Millau Viaduct 42
Designed to disappear into the landscape, this bridge is an engineering marvel.

We Thought 46

What Do You Think? 47

Index 48

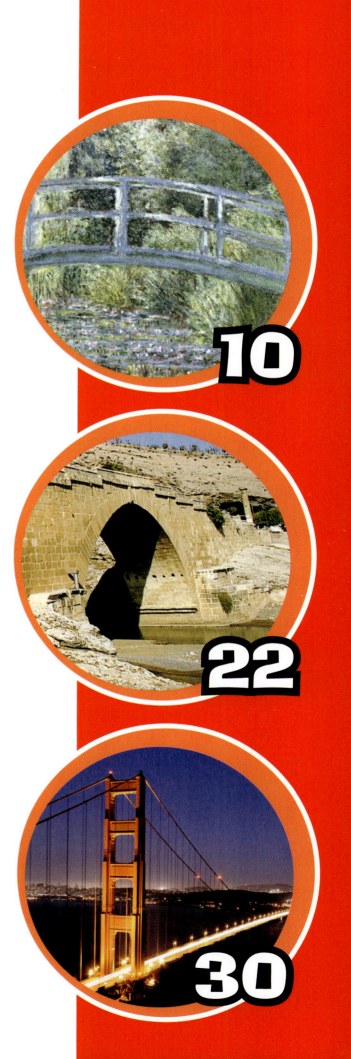

NOW WE'RE GETTING SOMEWHERE!

Have you hugged a bridge today? Just think of the hundreds of hours that you have saved thanks to your friendly neighborhood bridge. They cross rivers, highways, valleys … but they also do a lot more than get you from A to B.

Bridges don't have to be those boring concrete blobs that you barely know you are crossing. They can be marvels of engineering (or massive mistakes). They can be breathtakingly beautiful. They can be strong enough to tell nature to take a hike or old enough to have seen the days when people were fed to lions for entertainment.

Building bridges isn't easy. You've got to think like an engineer and consider budgets, safety, and don't forget style! (Life's too short to look at ugly bridges.) In this book we focus on the 10 most amazing bridges in the world. The three basic types of bridges — arch, beam, and suspension — are featured. We selected and ranked each bridge for its engineering feat, special features, artistic design, and construction challenges. We also thought about what the bridge means to people and why it is remembered.

Now's the time to put on your hard hat and ask yourself …

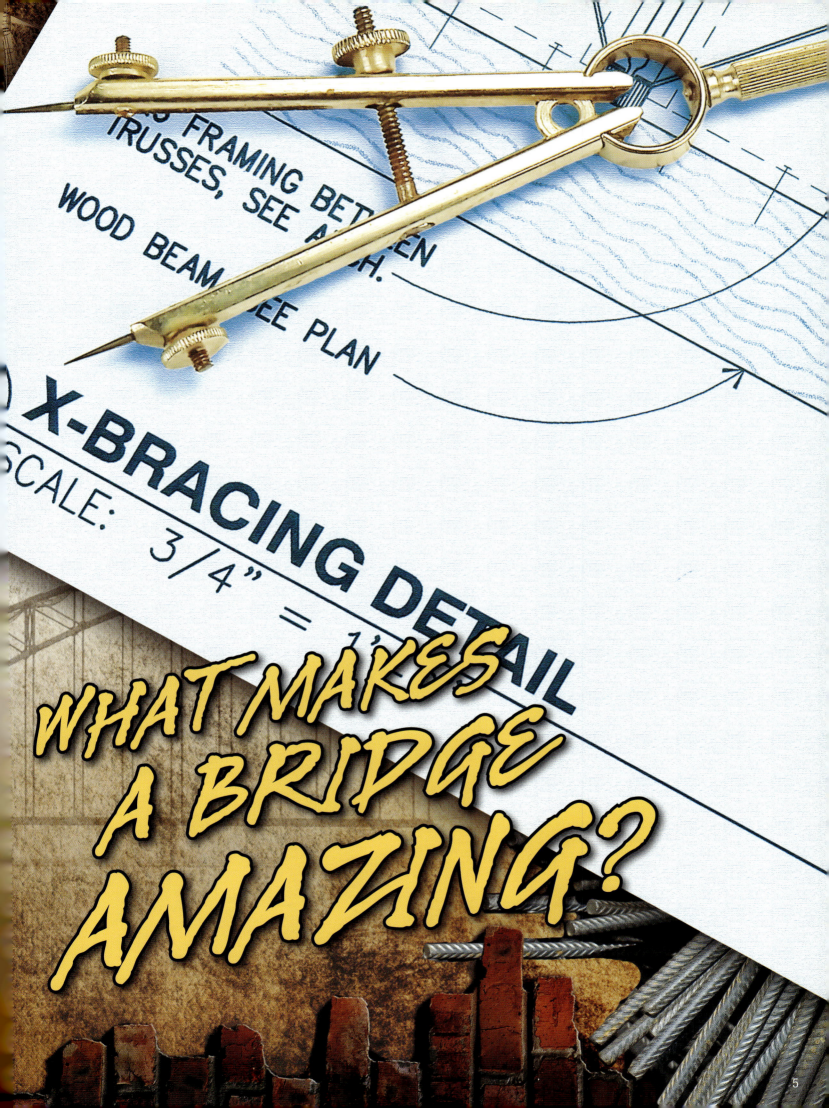
WHAT MAKES A BRIDGE AMAZING?

10 RAINBOW BRI

An arch bridge uses the strength of a semicircle to carry the load. The arch allows the weight on the bridge to be absorbed by the arch supports.

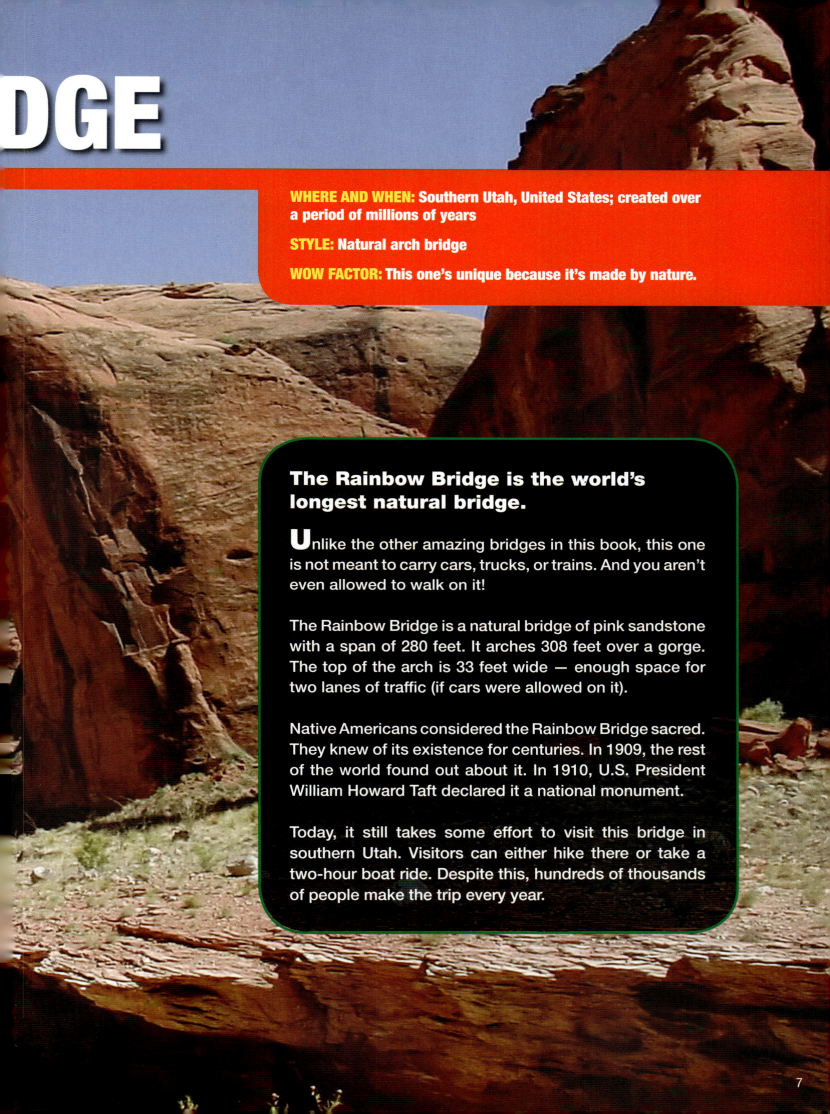

DGE

WHERE AND WHEN: Southern Utah, United States; created over a period of millions of years

STYLE: Natural arch bridge

WOW FACTOR: This one's unique because it's made by nature.

The Rainbow Bridge is the world's longest natural bridge.

Unlike the other amazing bridges in this book, this one is not meant to carry cars, trucks, or trains. And you aren't even allowed to walk on it!

The Rainbow Bridge is a natural bridge of pink sandstone with a span of 280 feet. It arches 308 feet over a gorge. The top of the arch is 33 feet wide — enough space for two lanes of traffic (if cars were allowed on it).

Native Americans considered the Rainbow Bridge sacred. They knew of its existence for centuries. In 1909, the rest of the world found out about it. In 1910, U.S. President William Howard Taft declared it a national monument.

Today, it still takes some effort to visit this bridge in southern Utah. Visitors can either hike there or take a two-hour boat ride. Despite this, hundreds of thousands of people make the trip every year.

Rainbow Bridge

WHERE IT STANDS
The Rainbow Bridge is located 12 miles northwest of Navajo Mountain in southern Utah. This is canyon country and there is no road from the mountain to the bridge.

Quick Fact
Up until the 1800s, Rainbow Bridge was known only to native people and a few beaver trappers, prospectors, and cowboys.

NEWSFLASH
The Rainbow Bridge can be reached by a two-hour boat ride on Lake Powell and a short walk. Lake Powell is an artificial lake that was created in the '60s when the Glen Canyon dam was built. The lake destroyed many Native American religious sites. In 1974, the Navajo tribe filed a lawsuit in the U.S. District Court hoping to protect their religious sites from destruction. The court ruled against them, saying that the need for water storage was more important than anything else.

 Do you think this was the right ruling? Why or why not?

Quick Fact
Visiting the Rainbow Bridge became easier after World War II. Surplus rubber rafts from the war became available for public use. Even with rafts, the trip down the Colorado River took several days and was followed by a seven-mile hike.

ENGINEERING FEAT
The Rainbow Bridge started out as a wall of sandstone, which had been built up in layers over millions of years. Some of the layers were soft sandstone and some were hard. Over the years, the water of the creek under the bridge wore away the softer sandstone layer at the base. This created a hole in the wall of sandstone. As the hole widened, an arch began to form.

SEEING IS BELIEVING
The local Native tribes consider the bridge sacred. Today, the National Park Service requests visitors to be respectful of the site. They ask tourists to stay within a restricted viewing area.

Quick Fact
The Paiute and Navajo tribes named the bridge *Nonnezoshe*, which means "rainbow turned to stone." In Navajo culture, the rainbow is a symbol of the guardian of the universe.

Over millions of years, weather and water erosion created a hole in the wall of sandstone. Slowly, as the hole widened, it formed a natural arch.

NATURAL WONDERS

The Rainbow Bridge isn't the only natural arch around. Read this Q&A to find out about others.

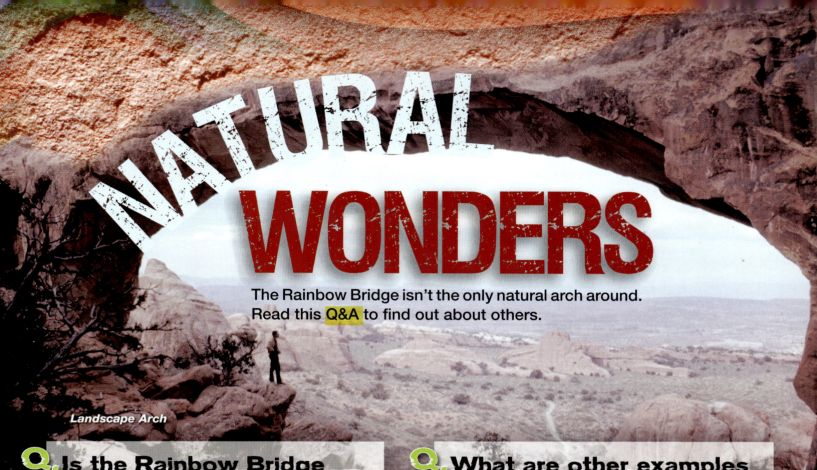

Landscape Arch

Q. Is the Rainbow Bridge the biggest natural arch?

A. No. Two arches, also in southern Utah, are longer. The Kolob Arch and Landscape Arch are several feet longer than the Rainbow Bridge. But, at 290 feet tall, the Rainbow Bridge towers over both of these. However, the world's tallest natural arch is Tushuk Tash in China (it comes in at a whopping 1,200 feet!).

Q. What are other examples of natural bridges?

A. The Sipapu, Kachina, and Owachomu are natural bridges. They are found in Natural Bridges National Monument in southeast Utah. The trail to these bridges passes by waterfalls and pools deep enough for swimming. You can't miss the Owachomu, the most spectacular of the three bridges. It is also the oldest bridge in the park.

The Expert Says…

" Had the Pleistocene climate pattern not [eased], the bridge might very well have thinned to the point of either snapping under its own weight or being unable to tolerate seismic activity. "

— David Kent Sproul, author of *A Bridge Between Cultures: An Administrative History of Rainbow Bridge National Monument*

Pleistocene: *period also known as the Ice Age, which began about 1.6 million years ago and ended about 11,000 years ago*

 Besides seismic activity caused by earthquakes, what are other concerns for bridge designers and engineers?

Take Note

Nature took millions of years to create the Rainbow Bridge. It is not meant for use, but this natural bridge, with its graceful arch, is design at its finest. For being a natural treasure, it deserves a place in our book of amazing bridges.
• Think of an amazing place you've visited or read about that you will always remember. What makes it unforgettable?

5   4   3   2   1

9 MONET'S BRI

It's easy to see why Claude Monet found his garden so inspiring. This bridge is the focal point of some of his best paintings.

...DGE

WHERE AND WHEN: Giverny, France; 1880s

STYLE: Arched wooden bridge with railings

WOW FACTOR: This bridge and its surroundings were so beautiful that they inspired artist Claude Monet to paint a series of masterpieces.

Monet's Bridge is the most famous bridge of its kind in the world.

What's so hot about a plain, green wooden bridge in a garden? In most gardens, absolutely nothing! But this wooden bridge happens to be in Claude Monet's garden. The famous Impressionist artist made 18 paintings of this bridge, which can be seen in galleries around the world.

Monet wanted to recreate a small bit of Japan, so he built a Japanese water garden. The pond and the bridge it crossed became an outdoor studio. Monet painted here every day, even when his eyesight began to fail.

Monet's painting *Le Bassin aux Nymphéas* (Water-Lily Pond) is one of his most recognizable pieces. The paintings he did of the bridge have been reproduced on everything from mugs and placemats to blankets and T-shirts.

MONET'S BRIDGE

Quick Fact
Monet designed his garden like a painting. He even had the flowers planted to follow a specific color pattern.

WHERE IT STANDS
This famous little bridge stands in Claude Monet's garden in the small French village of Giverny. It's about a one-hour train ride from Paris. If you want to take a picture of the Japanese bridge without tourists in the background, don't visit during the summer.

ENGINEERING FEAT
The structure is modeled on bridges found in traditional Japanese gardens. It is made of wood. Monet hired a Japanese gardener to help him recreate the style of a Japanese garden. He diverted water from a stream, the Ru, to run through his property. His neighbors were not pleased. They were afraid his strange foreign plants might poison the water.

NEWSFLASH
In 1926, Monet's son inherited the house and gardens at Giverny, but never lived there. After World War II, the property was in bad shape. In 1966, the Académie des Beaux-Arts, a French historical organization, took it over. Sadly, the bridge was too damaged to be saved. It had to be rebuilt.

? Why is it important to preserve a bridge as simple in design as this one?

SEEING IS BELIEVING
Monet's house and garden have become a popular tourist attraction. In the summer, the wooden railings of the bridge are covered with blossoms that hang heavily over the pond. Between April and October each year, about 500,000 people stroll through the garden and pause on the Japanese bridge to take in the beauty that Claude Monet captured in so many of his paintings.

Monet's house in Giverny

The Expert Says...
"Other famous bridges impose themselves on the landscape. They say, 'Look how we humans have conquered nature.' Monet's bridge sits perfectly in nature. It is there, but not there. Anyone who knows Monet's paintings wants to stand on that bridge."

— B. Sheppard, art teacher

? Why might some people be impressed by a bridge that blends into its surroundings? What would impress you more, Monet's Bridge or something larger? Explain your reasoning to a friend.

Bridge Through Time

Water-Lily Pond, Symphony in Green, 1899

Look closely at these two paintings Monet created of his Japanese bridge. Notice how they change as he gets older and his vision fails.

Monet's paintings of the bridge became looser and more and more abstract until eventually it was as if the bridge dissolved into nature.

abstract: *unrealistic*

? Which of the paintings on this page appeals to you more? Why?

The Japanese bridge on the water-lily pond at Giverny, 1924–25

Take Note

Like the Rainbow Bridge at #10, Monet's Bridge is beautiful and original. It attracts even more tourists and visitors from all over the world. In addition, this bridge lives on forever in Monet's paintings, and will be admired by future generations. For all these reasons, it is #9 on our list.
- Why do you think Monet's Bridge is so popular among tourists? If you were an engineer, would you be impressed? Why or why not?

5 4 3 2 1

8 KAWARAU BR

The Kawarau Bridge's engineer was able to design it in just 16 days. Even with today's technology, it would take at least six months to come up with the design!

WHERE AND WHEN: Queenstown, South Island, New Zealand; 1880

STYLE: Suspension bridge

WOW FACTOR: Kawarau (Ka-warra) is the first commercial bungee jumping bridge in the world.

The Kawarau Bridge is a hot spot for thrill-seekers.

This bridge is old — it was built in the 1880s to link Queenstown to Central Otago during New Zealand's gold rush. If only the gold miners could see it now! Today, people come to the bridge for a very different reason. With large rubber bands around their legs, they hurl themselves off the bridge into the spectacular Kawarau Gorge. The Kawarau Bridge is now more famous for bungee jumping than for its history.

The Kawarau is a 300-foot-long suspension bridge. This type of bridge has a deck supported by cables that are attached to two towers. In the most common type of suspension bridge, the cables are anchored at either end of the bridge and strung between the towers to form the shape of an M.

The bungee dive into the gorge is 143 feet — almost half the length of a football field. Options for a dive include a foot tie, a harness, a head and shoulder "splash-down" into the river, and tandem jumps if you want to go with a friend.

Imagine what those miners would think if they could see how their bridge is being used today!

KAWARAU BRIDGE

WHERE IT STANDS
The Kawarau Bridge is located 13 miles outside Queenstown, a tourist town on South Island, New Zealand. The geography of the Queenstown area makes it perfect for sports fanatics. Once a remote location, the bridge is now so close to the main highway that motorists can see bungee jumpers as they drive by.

ENGINEERING FEAT
The construction of the Kawarau Bridge was not easy. Materials had to be transported over 175 miles of railroad, 25 miles of water, and 12 miles of road. Originally, the design called for two tunnels to be created for the bridge anchors, one on the west side and one on the east side. But because of a dip in the rock on the east side, one of the shafts had to be sunk vertically.

Some of the stones used in the towers weigh two or more tons.

Quick Fact
The 28 steel cables that suspend the bridge were stretched and adjusted separately to the correct length. It took six working days to get the adjustments right.

NEWSFLASH
The Kawarau Bridge was closed to traffic in 1963 when a new arch bridge was built nearby. It was left to rot. If it hadn't been for the bungee jumping business, the bridge would have been torn down.

? What are some reasons, other than bungee jumping, that would make it important to preserve an old bridge?

SEEING IS BELIEVING
A.J. Hackett and Henry van Asch got permission from the conservation department to start bungee jumping from the old bridge. Since 1988, more than one million people have taken the plunge from the bridge.

Quick Fact
New Zealand has more bridges per capita than any other country in the world.

per capita: *for every person*

The Expert Says...
"For a structure of such significance, a modern design process would require at least 16 days to ensure the site location was the best, let alone produce a final design and construction drawings! Typically a modern fast track design process for a bridge such as the one spanning the Kawarau Gorge would take a minimum of six months, possibly as long as 12 months."

— Warren Batchelar, civil engineer

Down to a Science: Bungee Jumping

There's a lot more to bungee jumping than meets the eye. Check out this labeled diagram for the science behind this exciting sport. …

The Basics:
These are the three forces that come into play before, during, and after a jump …

Gravitational Potential Energy (GPE): The amount of energy an object (bungee jumper) has in relation to its height above the ground.

Kinetic Energy (KE): The energy that is possessed by a moving object (bungee jumper).

Elastic Potential Energy (EPE): The energy stored in a stretchy object (the bungee cord). The further the object is stretched, the more EPE it has.

1. As a jumper gathers the courage to jump, gravitational potential energy comes into play. This is stored energy that an object has due to its position above the Earth. The heavier jumpers are and the higher they are, the more gravitational potential energy they have.

2. As the jumper falls, the gravitational potential energy turns into kinetic energy.

3. The point where the jumper's cord reaches its total length before it starts to stretch is called the point of equilibrium. After the cord stretches past this point, the force changes to elastic potential energy.

4. Once the cord has stretched as far as it can, the elastic potential energy then becomes kinetic energy again.

5. As the jumper bounces up and down, the energy changes back and forth from kinetic energy to elastic potential energy.

kinetic: *connected with motion*

Diagram labels:
1. Standing on bridge: GPE
2. Jumping off bridge: KE
3. Point of equilibrium: EPE
4. Full length: KE
5. Bouncing: KE to EPE

Take Note
Like Monet's Bridge, the Kawarau Bridge is getting a whole lot of attention but for a very different reason. For its historic importance and its record as the first bungee jumping bridge in the world, the Kawarau Bridge jumps to the #8 spot on our list, ahead of Monet's Bridge.
- How do the Kawarau Bridge and the Monet Bridge affect tourism for New Zealand and France?

7 QUEBEC BRID

A beam bridge's weight is fully supported by the piers at either end of it. The weight of the bridge pushes straight down on the piers. So, the longer it is, the weaker the bridge becomes.

WHERE AND WHEN: The St. Lawrence River in Quebec, Canada; 1919

STYLE: Cantilever (modified beam bridge)

WOW FACTOR: It is the longest cantilever bridge in the world, but it is remembered for two tragic accidents that happened during its construction.

Almost 90 workers died during the construction of this bridge.

Cutting costs is not always a good thing — especially when it comes to building bridges. And when an engineer's ego gets in the way of common sense and training, it's a disaster.

The Quebec Bridge is remembered as the site of the worst bridge disaster in the history of Canada. Theodore Cooper was the consulting engineer on the project. When he was told that some of the joints were not closing and that the workers were having trouble **riveting** them together, Cooper said, "It is not serious." He was wrong.

On August 29, 1907, one of the bridge's huge steel spans plunged into the river with many workers on it. Of those who fell, 75 died. The youngest casualty was a 14-year-old boy. A second disaster occurred on September 11, 1916, killing 11 workers. The bridge was finally completed in 1919 at a total cost of more than $21 million.

---

riveting: *fastening with rivets (rivets are like gigantic nails)*

QUEBEC BRIDGE

WHERE IT STANDS
The Quebec Bridge crosses the St. Lawrence River. It is located six miles from Quebec City. The St. Lawrence River runs very deep, which is one of the reasons the consulting engineer decided to move the supporting piers closer to the banks of the river.

ENGINEERING FEAT
The Quebec Bridge is a cantilever bridge. A cantilever bridge has spans or arms that are attached to piers and project out over the water. These spans are joined by a beam bridge in the middle. This design allows for longer spans and higher bridges. The part of the bridge that collapsed in 1907 was made of 19,000 tons of steel. Cooper underestimated the weight of all the materials — known as the "dead weight" — by 4,000 tons. This extra weight caused the steel ribs to bend and eventually collapse.

NEWSFLASH
After the first accident, a different engineer was hired and the design was changed. But disaster struck again. On September 11, 1916, just as the bridge's center span was being lifted into place, one of the four rocker arms designed to hold it up failed. The span fell into the river, killing 11 workers.

SEEING IS BELIEVING
Today the bridge carries pedestrians, vehicles, and trains across the St. Lawrence River. With a total length of 3,238 feet and a span measuring 1,800 feet, the Quebec Bridge still has the longest cantilevered span in the world. Many people still wonder if that record was worth the human toll.

Quick Fact: When engineers graduate from Canadian universities, they receive an iron ring. Although rumor has it that early graduates' rings were made from the wreckage of the Quebec Bridge, it is not true.

Quick Fact: The computer technology we have today would have allowed Theodore Cooper to run tests on the design. He would have quickly found out that the bridge was too heavy to hold.

Quick Fact: The next longest cantilever bridge is the Forth Bridge in Scotland. Its two longest spans are 1,710 feet each.

Collapse of the center span of the Quebec Bridge in 1916

The Quebec Bridge Disaster of 1907

Discover the shocking truth in this article…

"There was this tremor like an earthquake and a roar. Then this bad grinding sound and a thunder as the bridge fell into the water."

— John Montour, an iron worker on the bridge

Wreckage from Quebec Bridge disaster, 1907

Theodore Cooper, the consulting engineer on the project, was worried there wouldn't be enough money to complete the bridge. Among the cost-cutting measures he made was one that came with deadly results: he increased the middle span length from 1,600 feet to 1,800 feet so the piers would be closer to shore. He claimed that by doing this the piers would be less open to dangerous ice floes. The reality was that it would cut the cost and time involved to get things done.

The bridge collapsed, killing 75 men, many of them high-steel workers from the Caughnawaga Reservation. Close to a dozen men were pinned under the wreckage that had fallen onto the tidal flats at the edge of the river. Bystanders watched helplessly as the tide came in, drowning the trapped men.

About 40 bodies were never recovered and are probably still trapped in the steel wreckage that took them to their deaths.

What lessons can engineers learn from the Quebec Bridge disaster?

The Expert Says…

"It took only fifteen seconds for the massive south arm of the Quebec Bridge to fall into the St. Lawrence River in 1907, but the prelude to the catastrophe began years before."

— John Tarkov, author of *A Disaster in the Making*

Take Note

This bridge taught engineers around the world about the importance of accuracy and precision. Even today, many engineering students study what went wrong with the Quebec Bridge so they won't repeat the same mistakes. For what it has taught us, we rank it #7 on our list of most amazing bridges.

- Think about what it takes to be involved in the construction of a bridge or skyscraper. What makes these workers special?

6 CENDERE BRI

They don't build them like they used to! Can you imagine one of today's bridges lasting for over 1,000 years?

DGE

WHERE AND WHEN: Spanning the Kahta River in Turkey; built in the 2nd century

STYLE: Stone arch bridge

WOW FACTOR: Cendere (Jehn-dehr) is still going strong at 1,800 years of age.

It is one of the oldest known bridges in the world.

How would your bones be holding up if you were 1,800 years old? That's how old the Cendere Bridge in Turkey is, and it's holding up just fine.

This bridge was built in Roman times, and it is still in use today. The Romans certainly knew how to build things to last. They used the stone arch design for many structures, from doorways to vaulted roofs and giant aqueducts. They were famous for their arched bridges that could support the weight of giant armies in full battle gear, together with their carts, supplies, and horses.

The Cendere Bridge has one single arch. The bridge's span is 112 feet and its length is 394 feet. There are three decorative columns, two at one end of the bridge and one at the other. These columns are almost 33 feet high.

The Romans built the Cendere Bridge to honor Emperor Septimius Severus, his wife, and sons. It is also known as the Severan Bridge.

CENDERE BRIDGE

WHERE IT STANDS
The Cendere Bridge is 34 miles from Adiyaman (Ah-dee-ah-mahn), Turkey. Turkey straddles Europe and Asia. Adiyaman is in the southeastern part of the country, not far from Iraq. The Cendere Bridge crosses the narrowest part of the Kahta River.

ENGINEERING FEAT
The Romans had figured out the secret of cement-making very early on. They mixed slaked lime (prepared by combining calcium oxide with water) and pozzolana, a volcanic ash from Mount Vesuvius. The cement that resulted was capable of hardening underwater. Unlike the Rainbow Bridge, which was carved by nature, the Cendere Bridge was built by soldiers in Legion XVI (Legion 16). The arch consists of 92 stones, each weighing about 10 tons.

straddles: *stretches from one place to the other*

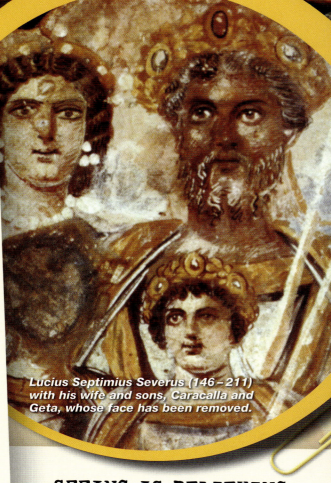

Lucius Septimius Severus (146–211) with his wife and sons, Caracalla and Geta, whose face has been removed.

NEWSFLASH
There were originally four decorative columns on the bridge, two dedicated to Emperor Septimius Severus and his wife, and two columns dedicated to their sons, Caracalla and Geta. After Caracalla murdered his brother, he ordered Geta's column to be destroyed. He didn't want anything around to remind him of Geta.

SEEING IS BELIEVING
The Cendere Bridge was restored in 1997. Today, vehicles weighing up to five tons are allowed to go across it. Traffic isn't much of a worry though because there is a modern road bridge less than a third of a mile away.

? Why would it be important to restore the bridge? Come up with three reasons.

Quick Fact
It was common for bridges to be built by soldiers while they were waiting for battle. Although Roman bridges were built by soldiers, they were maintained by slaves.

What other things can you think of that were built long ago, but can still be used today? **?**

The Expert Says...
" Old bridges such as the Cendere Bridge … are a good lesson to modern engineers that you don't need computers and modern equipment to design and build structures that will function extremely well and last a long time. "
— Warren Batchelar, civil engineer

BUILT TO LAST

This labeled diagram of an arch bridge will take a load off your mind.

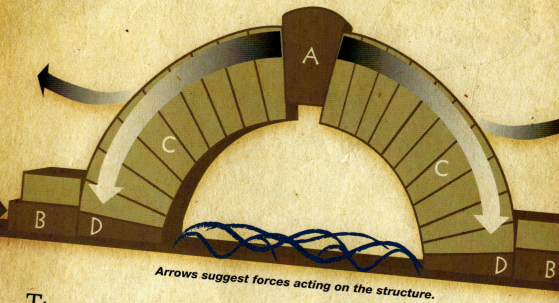

Arrows suggest forces acting on the structure.

This arch bridge is constructed from wedge-shaped stones (voussoirs) that are cut to fit together and form a semicircle. The stone in the center or top of the arch is called the keystone. Abutments (supporting structures) at the ends of the bridge keep the bridge from flattening out when weight is added to the top of the arch by the bridge materials, the road surface, and the traffic that crosses it.

The diagram on this page shows how the arch bridge works. The keystone is pushed downward by the weight of the load. Because it is wedge-shaped, it pushes outward to the voussoirs on either side of it. So, while it may seem that the weight would push straight down, the load is spread out sideways, around the edge of the arch and into the ground. The abutments push in against the stones, keeping the arch from spreading and the central section from collapsing inward.

LEGEND
A- Keystone
B- Abutments
C- Voussoirs
D- Footers

Take Note

The Cendere Bridge was built long before builders had fancy tools and advanced design theories. But engineers still use the basic principle of the keystone. Coming in at #6 on our list, the Cendere Bridge teaches us that good design was invented long before modern engineering.
- Research online for more examples of stone arch bridges. Make a list of them under these headings: Name, Location, and Date of Construction.

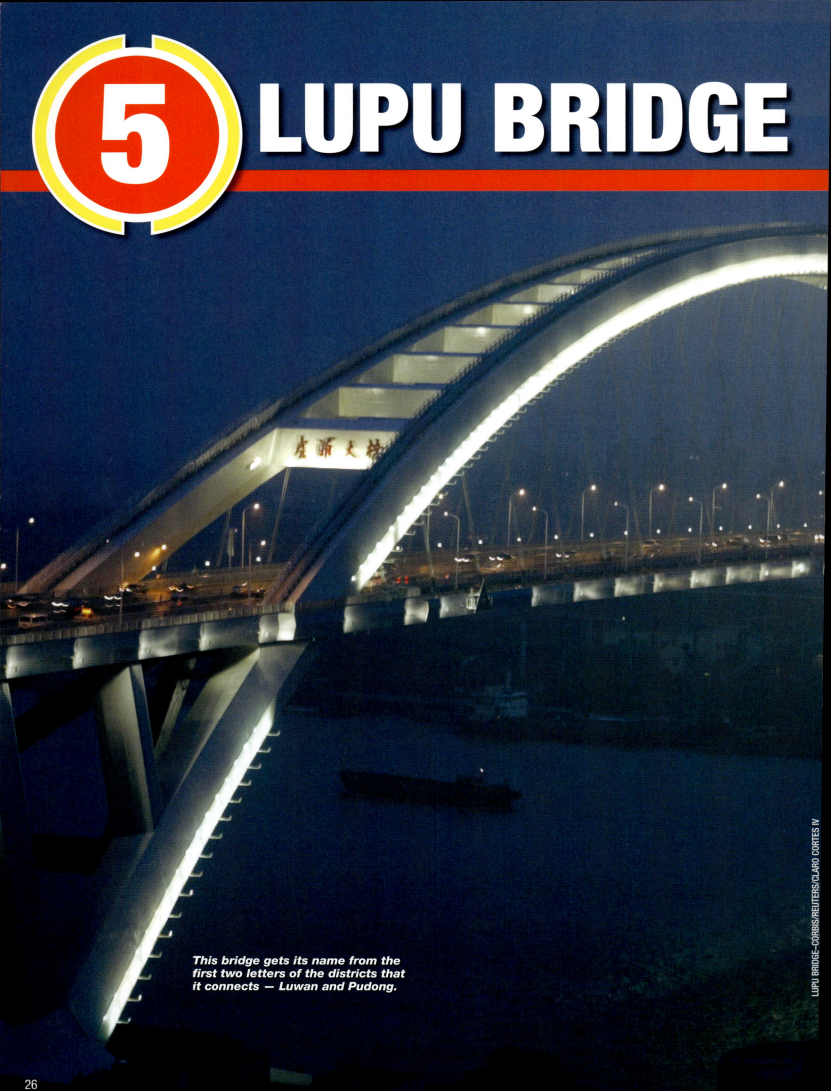

5 LUPU BRIDGE

This bridge gets its name from the first two letters of the districts that it connects — Luwan and Pudong.

WHERE AND WHEN: Shanghai, China; 2003

STYLE: Box arch bridge (the arch ribs are solid)

WOW FACTOR: It has a main span of 1,804 feet — making it the longest arch bridge in the world.

It has been called a "steel rainbow."

If size really does matter, then Shanghai's Lupu Bridge deserves to be high on our list of amazing bridges. Its main span stretches 1,804 feet (beating the previous record holder for longest span by a mere 105 feet!). Also, there are no visible supports between the surface of the bridge and the river 164 feet below. Anyone with gephyrophobia (a fear of crossing bridges) is advised to avoid this bridge altogether!

The Lupu Bridge links two districts in Shanghai — Luwan on the north bank of the Huangpu River and Pudong on the south bank. It is an engineering feat that adds another impressive landmark to China's largest city.

Shanghai agreed to build the bridge as part of its bid to host Expo 2010, a major international event. Easing traffic congestion was an important consideration. Planners estimated that the fair would attract 70 million people. Imagine this number of visitors crossing the Lupu Bridge — that's almost twice the population of California!

LUPU BRIDGE

WHERE IT STANDS
The Lupu Bridge spans the Huangpu River in Shanghai, China.

ENGINEERING FEAT
The Lupu Bridge is made entirely of steel. It took 50,700 tons of steel to build it (about the same amount of steel needed to build 17,500 mid-sized SUVs), at a cost of $302 million. It took 770 tons of paint to coat the bridge. During a suspension test, 36 trucks, each carrying a 30-ton load, drove over the bridge at the same time. The bridge sank five inches, which is considered safe. Because the two piers of the Lupu Bridge stand on soft ground, eight construction research teams were hired to make the bridge safe, especially during earthquakes and tornadoes.

Quick Fact
The bridge can withstand an earthquake measuring 7.0 on the Richter scale. This is considered a major earthquake. It was also built to withstand hurricane-force winds.

The Expert Says...
"A bridge is predominantly designed to support vertical loads from traffic, which can be established reasonably accurately. Earthquakes, however, are unpredictable and the loads cannot be determined with any great accuracy. This generally results in the bridge structure being designed for a 'best guess' earthquake load and to allow for large sideward movements to absorb the energy from the earthquake load."

— Warren Batchelar, civil engineer

Yao Ming

New River Gorge Bridge

Quick Fact
The second longest arch bridge span, at about 2,000 feet, is the New River Gorge Bridge in West Virginia. It was completed in 1977 and cost $37 million.

NEWSFLASH
When the Lupu Bridge opened in June 2003, Chinese Basketball Association and NBA star Yao Ming led 1,000 people in a run across the bridge. There was plenty of room for the runners during the 2.4 mile run (the total length of the bridge) on the six-lane bridge.

? Why do you think Yao Ming was chosen to be part of the bridge opening? If you were to choose someone to represent your country at the opening of a record-breaking structure, who would it be and why?

SEEING IS BELIEVING
Each year, thousands of tourists take a high-speed, see-through elevator to the main deck of the bridge. They then climb 300 steps along the bridge's arched rib to get to a viewing platform located at the highest point of the arch. That platform is 328 feet above the water. Think of it this way — the highest a diving board at your local pool can be is 33 feet. Most local pools stick to 3-foot- and 10-foot-high boards.

LET'S COMPARE!

Just how huge is a 1,804-foot span? Have a look at this ==comparison chart== to put it all into perspective.

Lupu Bridge — 1,804 ft Span — Pier — Pier

CN Tower — 1,815 ft

Sears Tower — 1,450 ft

	Height/length	Common items relative to the length of the span of the Lupu Bridge
Yao Ming	7'6"	Yao Ming could flip head to toe 240 times before reaching the end of the span of the Lupu Bridge.
School bus	40 ft	Nearly 46 school buses could line the bridge span in single file.
Basketball court	94 ft	The bridge span is the length of about 19 basketball courts.

Quick Fact
The Lupu Bridge is almost 820 feet longer than the Eiffel Tower in Paris is tall. And it is 550 feet longer than the Empire State Building in New York City!

Take Note
While the Cendere Bridge at #6 is the oldest Roman arch bridge still in use, the Lupu Bridge is a modern engineering feat. It is the longest, newest, and most impressive arch bridge today, and was designed and built with ideas from eight teams of experts. It's in Shanghai, one of the most populated cities in the world, which attracts millions of overseas visitors each year. For these reasons, we've awarded it the #5 spot on our list.
- Which bridge would you visit, the Cendere Bridge or the Lupu Bridge? What would influence your choice?

4 GOLDEN GATE

A suspension bridge's deck is held up by cables, ropes, or chains. The cables are strung through tall towers. Those towers support most of the bridge's weight.

BRIDGE

WHERE AND WHEN: San Francisco, California; 1937

STYLE: Suspension bridge

WOW FACTOR: It was an engineering feat and it held the record for the longest suspension bridge in the world for 27 years.

The Golden Gate Bridge is one of the longest and most beautiful suspension bridges in the world.

The Golden Gate Bridge is recognized all over the world as a symbol of San Francisco. It is 1.7 miles long, with a main span of almost 4,200 feet. The cables that support the deck of the bridge are some of the longest and thickest bridge cables ever made. Each cable is 7,659 feet long and is made up of 27,572 parallel wires.

Building this bridge was no easy task. Major concerns were weather and earthquakes. The Bay Area experiences a lot of fog, rain, and high winds. As well, San Francisco sits on the San Andreas fault line where earthquakes are a real possibility.

GOLDEN GATE BRIDGE

WHERE IT STANDS
The Golden Gate Bridge connects the city of San Francisco to Marin County (near Sausalito). It spans the Golden Gate Strait, which is where San Francisco Bay opens into the Pacific Ocean.

ENGINEERING FEAT
Workers used over one million tons of concrete to build the huge blocks that hold the bridge's cables. Workers had to do their jobs in high winds, 220 to 745 feet above the water. Metal surfaces were often slippery-wet because of the fog, making construction work really dangerous. So for safety's sake, during construction, Engineer Joseph Strauss spent $130,000 on netting that ran underneath the bridge. The bridge was completed in 1937 at a cost of $27 million.

SEEING IS BELIEVING
This beautiful and imposing structure is a must-see for tourists. It was painted red to make it visible in foggy weather and to make it blend with the natural surroundings. It is one of the most photographed bridges in the world. It has been written about in songs and books, and is featured in movies and television shows.

NEWSFLASH
In 2006, the Golden Gate Bridge, Highway and Transportation District, approved a study on the effects of building a safety barrier on the Golden Gate Bridge. Opponents say it will be difficult to design a barrier that does not add wind stress to the bridge.

During construction, the safety net below the bridge saved the lives of the 19 workers who had fallen at different times from the bridge.

BRIDGING THE GOLDEN GATE

History is filled with numbers. This **fact chart** highlights some of the Golden Gate Bridge's most important ones.

1933
the year actual construction of the bridge began

11
the number of men who lost their lives during the construction

From **$4** to **$11**
the daily wages for a construction worker on the bridge. The work was dangerous and difficult but the workers were happy to have jobs (it was built during the Great Depression).

200,000
the approximate number of people who walked on the bridge on the day it was opened to pedestrians

1,779,032,891
the number of vehicles that have crossed the bridge since June 2005

The bridge is 1.7 miles long.

The Expert Says…

"If [the safety barrier is] not designed correctly, however, the addition to the bridge could result in the bridge being overloaded under wind loads and cause some damage to the bridge structure."

— Warren Batchelar, civil engineer

Take Note

The Golden Gate Bridge is an unmistakable landmark of San Francisco. It is an important highway for the city, carrying hundreds of thousands of vehicles and pedestrians each day. For its impressive looks and remarkable history, we rank this bridge #4 on our list.
- List the challenges that engineers had to overcome during construction and compare them with other bridges on our list.

5   4   3   2   1

3 LONDON BRIDGE

Are you wondering why there are palm trees in London? Well, that's because this London Bridge is in Arizona! It was taken apart in London and later rebuilt in Lake Havasu, Arizona.

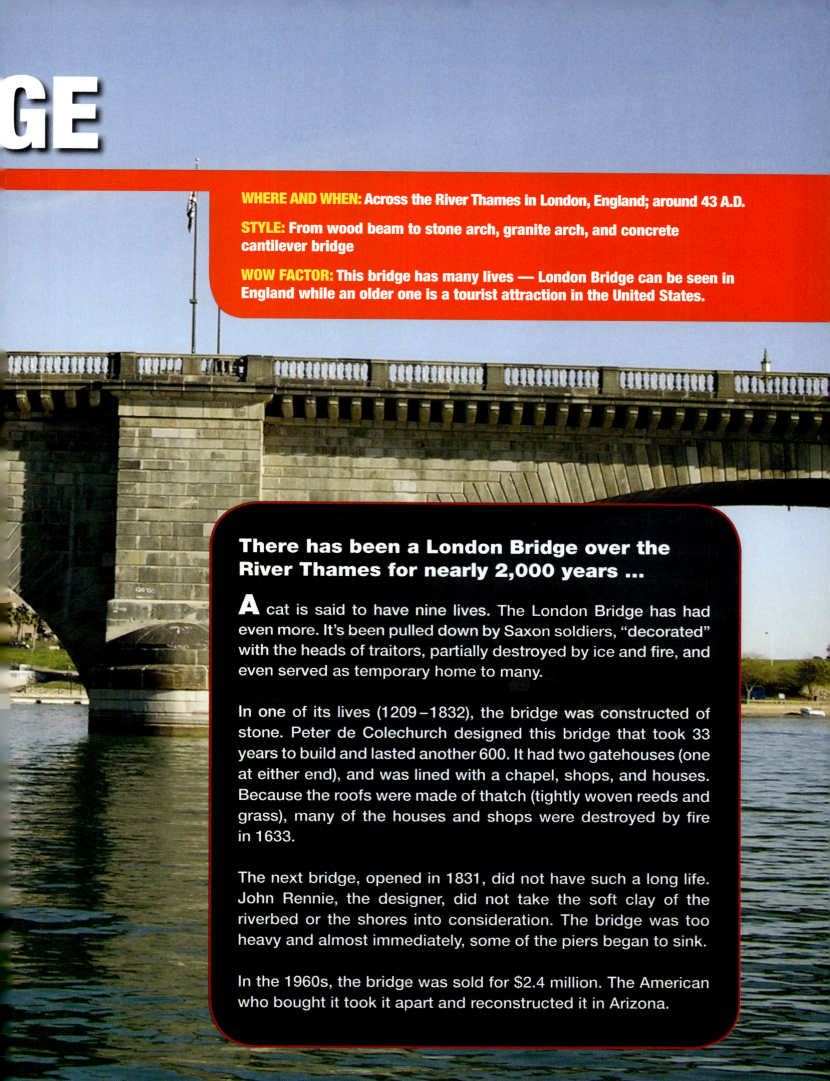

WHERE AND WHEN: Across the River Thames in London, England; around 43 A.D.

STYLE: From wood beam to stone arch, granite arch, and concrete cantilever bridge

WOW FACTOR: This bridge has many lives — London Bridge can be seen in England while an older one is a tourist attraction in the United States.

There has been a London Bridge over the River Thames for nearly 2,000 years …

A cat is said to have nine lives. The London Bridge has had even more. It's been pulled down by Saxon soldiers, "decorated" with the heads of traitors, partially destroyed by ice and fire, and even served as temporary home to many.

In one of its lives (1209–1832), the bridge was constructed of stone. Peter de Colechurch designed this bridge that took 33 years to build and lasted another 600. It had two gatehouses (one at either end), and was lined with a chapel, shops, and houses. Because the roofs were made of thatch (tightly woven reeds and grass), many of the houses and shops were destroyed by fire in 1633.

The next bridge, opened in 1831, did not have such a long life. John Rennie, the designer, did not take the soft clay of the riverbed or the shores into consideration. The bridge was too heavy and almost immediately, some of the piers began to sink.

In the 1960s, the bridge was sold for $2.4 million. The American who bought it took it apart and reconstructed it in Arizona.

LONDON BRIDGE

WHERE IT STANDS
London Bridge is in London, England. It is built across the River Thames. Although many bridges have been built over the centuries, they have all been located in almost the same place.

ENGINEERING FEAT
The early bridges (built sometime after the year 43) were constructed from wood and clay. These bridges were not durable and were rebuilt many times. The first stone bridge (1209–1832) was the longest lasting but even this was remodeled and repaired many times. Granite was used in the London Bridge completed in 1831. The newest bridge (built between 1967 and 1972) is made of concrete.

> **?** Which bridge would you have most liked to visit, the newest one or one of the older ones? Why?

NEWSFLASH
A chapel that was built on the first stone London Bridge had a crypt at water level. The designer of the bridge, Peter de Colechurch, died in 1205 before the bridge was finished and was buried in that crypt. His bones were found in the crypt when another London Bridge was being constructed in the 1820s. Unfortunately, they were dumped into the river.

Tower Bridge

Quick Fact
Did you think London Bridge looked like the photo above? This is actually London's Tower Bridge (many people wrongly think this is London Bridge).

SEEING IS BELIEVING
In Arizona, the granite arch London Bridge (1831–1968) attracts many tourists. To transport the bridge across the ocean, each stone was dismantled and carefully marked so that it could be reconstructed just as John Rennie had designed it. It took three years to rebuild the bridge in its new home.

> **?** Why is it important to save the history of a bridge such as the London Bridge?

Old London Bridge, 1630

Falling Down

*"London Bridge is falling down,
Falling down, falling down,
London Bridge is falling down,
My fair lady."*

This article reveals the truth behind the lyrics of one of the most popular nursery rhymes of all time.

This nursery rhyme was first written around the year 1000, probably with slightly different words. At that time, the Danes controlled London but bands of Saxons and Vikings joined together to capture the bridge and defeat the Danes. The Danes stood on the bridge throwing spears at the boats, but the Vikings had already thought of a plan. They protected themselves with thatched roofs they had ripped off the houses of local villagers, then rowed under the bridge, tied ropes to the wooden supports, and pulled the bridge down.

It wasn't until around 1269 that the song was rewritten with the words we know today. Back then, London Bridge was a toll bridge. The money collected traditionally went to keep the bridge in good repair. When Henry III came to power, he turned over the collected tolls to his wife who loved to shop. She spent all the money on herself and the bridge started to fall apart. The words of the song were revised as a criticism of her spending. The last line of the rhyme, "My fair lady," was likely a reference to the queen.

Over the centuries, London Bridge has been rebuilt many times. The modern London Bridge was completed in 1972 and opened by Queen Elizabeth II in 1973.

The Expert Says...

> Modern engineers use a detailed site investigation to find out what kind of soils are on the proposed site of the bridge. Included in the investigation would be a series of boreholes drilled into the earth to get samples of the soil, which would then be sent to a soils laboratory for extensive testing to find out how strong the materials are and how much load they can support.

— Warren Batchelar, civil engineer

Take Note

London Bridge is a symbol of London, England. It has endured many battles, a fire, a storm, and two world wars. Many people, young and old, will remember this bridge because of its famous song. For all these reasons, London Bridge takes the #3 spot on our list of most amazing bridges.

- What arguments would you make to agree or disagree with the strong finish of London Bridge on our list? Compare this bridge with any one of the bridges you have read about so far.

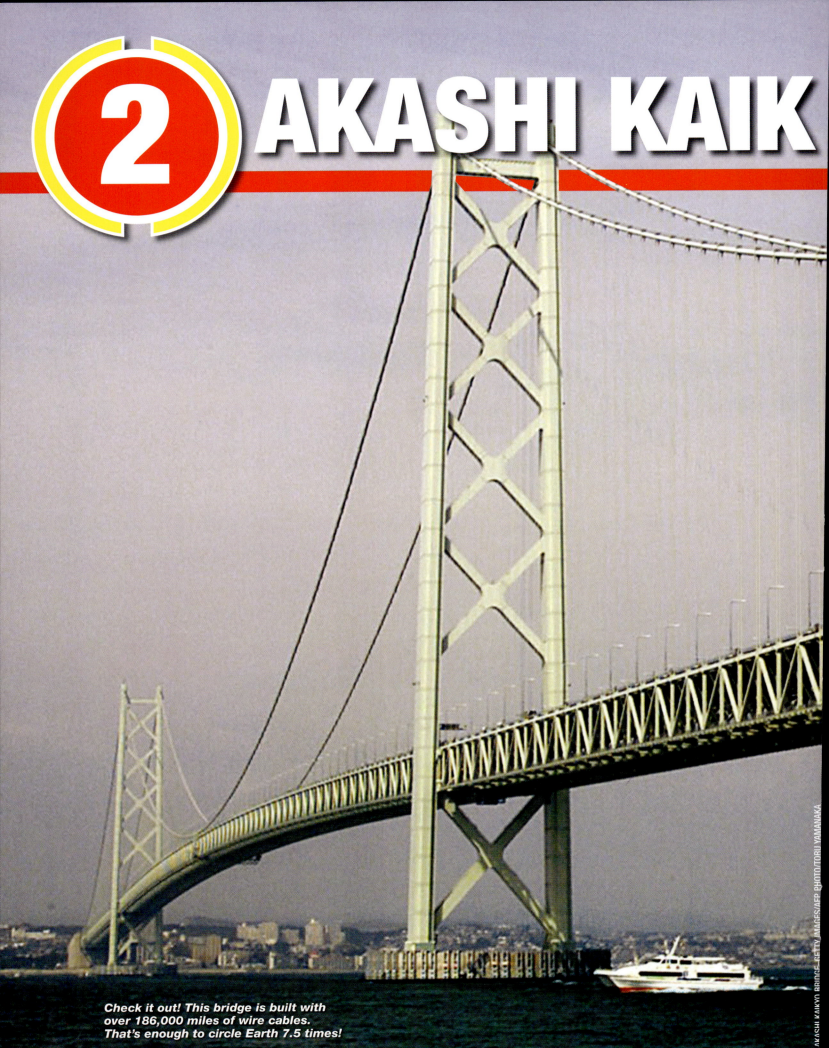

② AKASHI KAIK

Check it out! This bridge is built with over 186,000 miles of wire cables. That's enough to circle Earth 7.5 times!

YO BRIDGE

WHERE AND WHEN: Honshu and Awaji islands, Japan; 1998

STYLE: Suspension bridge

WOW FACTOR: The Akashi Kaikyo (Ak-kah-shee Kay-key-oh) is built to last — during construction it survived an earthquake of 7.2 on the Richter scale.

A gold medal winner!

If there was an event for bridge engineering in the Olympics, the Akashi Kaikyo Bridge would easily win four gold medals. The first three medals would be awarded for its spectacular engineering. It is currently the longest, tallest, and most expensive suspension bridge in the world. The fourth medal would be awarded for its safety record — there were no work-related deaths during its construction.

The Akashi Kaikyo Bridge even survived an enormous earthquake once. Maybe it was the expert construction of the 213-foot-high (33 stories) steel caissons that kept the bridge towers from falling. Or maybe it was the two 200-ton anchors that held the cables in position.

This bridge was also built to survive some of the most extreme weather in the world. The bridge deck is supported with a truss (a network of triangular braces) that the wind can blow straight through. The Akashi Strait is whipped by strong winds, sometimes up to 180 miles per hour in a typhoon, and heavy rains, up to 57 inches per year.

Whatever the challenge, this bridge is ready and prepared to put on a gold medal performance.

caissons: *structures used to build piers under water*

AKASHI KAIKYO BRIDGE

WHERE IT STANDS

The Akashi Kaikyo Bridge is located in Japan. It connects two islands: Awaji (the sixth largest in Japan) and Honshu (the largest island in Japan). It forms one part of the Kobe-Naruto expressway that transports millions of people back and forth from Honshu, where Japan's capital, Tokyo, is located, to the southern island of Shikoku.

ENGINEERING FEAT

The main span (the distance between the central piers) is 6,530 feet long, making it the current longest suspension bridge in the world. The total length of the bridge is 2.4 miles. Each of the two cables supporting the bridge is made up of 37,000 strands of steel wire that run the full length of the bridge. In all, there are 186,000 miles of cabling.

> **?** Why would each cable need to be made up of so many strands of steel wire?

Quick Fact
It took two million workers and 10 years to construct the bridge.

NEWSFLASH

On January 17, 1995, Japan was hit by a huge earthquake. The bridge was designed to withstand an earthquake measuring 8.5 on the Richter scale with an *epicenter* 90 miles away. This earthquake measured 7.2, but its epicenter was only 2.5 miles away! Luckily, the deck of the bridge had not been built. During the earthquake, the bridge could shake and move with little damage.

epicenter: where an earthquake starts

SEEING IS BELIEVING

Think of how you mix colors for a painting. An unusual system of lights made up of 1,092 special lighting units has been attached above the main suspension cable on the Akashi Kaikyo Bridge. Each one of the units can mix red, blue, and green light to paint a rainbow of colors across the night sky.

Quick Fact
The earthquake caused one of the bridge's towers to shift from its original spot. Because it was the foundation that moved, the structure on top would merely have followed the movement of the foundation and shifted to its new position. Engineers found that despite the shift, no damage had been sustained.

The Expert Says...

" It is estimated that the [earthquake] damages would not have been this slight had the cables not been already installed. "

— Juhani Virola, ATSE (Australian Academy of Technological Sciences and Engineering)

SHAKE, rattle, and ROLL
EARTHQUAKES TAKE THEIR TOLL

In the battle of earthquake versus bridge, who will be left standing? Find out in this **fact chart**.

	Location	Year	Size (Richter scale)	Damage
Million Dollar Bridge	Alaska, U.S.	1964	8.1	The bridge was knocked off its supports.
Shi Wei Bridge	Taiwan	1999	7.6	Piers tilted, causing spans on the bridge to collapse.
Akashi Kaikyo Bridge	Japan (unfinished at the time of the quake)	1995	7.2	One of the towers and its anchors moved, increasing the overall length of the finished bridge.
San Francisco Oakland Bay Bridge	California, U.S.	1989	6.9	A section of the upper road deck collapsed onto the deck below.
Rio Dulce Bridge	Guatemala	1999	6.7	Supports at either end of the flying span collapsed.

San Francisco Oakland Bay Bridge

Take Note

The London Bridge survived some pretty nasty attacks, but nothing could compare to the impact of an earthquake measuring 7.2 on the Richter scale. This bridge is built to withstand destructive natural forces: earthquakes, typhoons, heavy rain, and tidal currents. This is why it takes the #2 spot on our list.
- Describe the Akashi Kaikyo Bridge in an e-mail to someone who has never heard about it. What details would you share?

5 4 3 **2** 1

1 MILLAU VIAD

The Millau Viaduct represents the perfect combination of form and function. It is considered one of the most impressive engineering feats of our time.

UCT

WHERE AND WHEN: Millau, France; 2004

STYLE: Cable-stayed bridge (a kind of suspension bridge)

WOW FACTOR: Millau (Mee-yoh) is currently the highest bridge in the world.

Don't fall off this bridge!

If you are afraid of heights — stay away from this bridge! The Millau Viaduct is 804 feet off the ground in some sections.

This bridge is a cable-stayed bridge, which is a type of suspension bridge. It has one or more towers and is supported by wires that come down from the towers in the shape of an A. It was designed by French bridge engineer Michel Virlogeux, who worked closely with British architect Norman Foster. Luckily for us, the team had nervous drivers in mind when they designed the bridge. They knew that if a bridge 804 feet high and 1.6 miles long were built in a straight line, drivers would feel like they were floating — not a good thing when you are that far off the ground! So they built it with a slight curve and a three percent slope to improve visibility and make drivers feel more comfortable.

The architect played a special role in this bridge design. It's meant to look delicate and almost transparent. The Millau Viaduct blends softly into the landscape and almost disappears against the horizon. The result is stunning and almost magical. Read on to find out why it is our choice for the most amazing bridge in the world.

***

viaduct: *long, raised roadway, usually over a valley*

MILLAU VIADUCT

The crane operator, who lifted concrete sections onto the piers, spent seven hours a day "like a bird between the sky and the ground." His crane had a den, toilet, and air conditioning.

WHERE IT STANDS

The Millau Viaduct is located in southern France. The bridge spans a gorge between two plateaus. Below it runs the River Tarn. This bridge was built to reduce traffic jams on the highway that stretches between Paris, France, and Barcelona, Spain.

ENGINEERING FEAT

What do you get for around $530 million? Over three million cubic feet of concrete, 5,500 tons of reinforced steel, and cutting-edge technology to put it all together. The bridge deck, which can carry up to six lanes of traffic, is held up by cables that are attached to seven vertical hollow concrete pillars, each shaped like an upside-down V. The bridge deck was constructed in 18 sections. Each section was pushed out toward the piers using hydraulic jacks. Talk about slow work! The farthest a section of the bridge could move in one push was 24 inches. It took four weeks to move one section into its proper place.

NEWSFLASH

The bridge opened on December 14, 2004. In its first year, it carried 4,430,000 vehicles — many more than had been estimated. To cover the construction costs of this bridge, all drivers have to pay a toll. The company that constructed the bridge is allowed by the French government to collect tolls for 75 years — until 2080.

SEEING IS BELIEVING

The span between each pier is 1,122 feet. The bridge's concrete piers range in height from 246 feet to 770 feet from road level. The cable-stays that hold up the bridge deck are guaranteed to remain in "good condition" for 120 years.

The Expert Says...

"A work of man must fuse with nature. The pillars had to look almost organic, like they had grown from the earth."

— Norman Foster, bridge architect

Do you agree with Norman Foster? Why or why not?

Quick Fact
At its highest point, the Millau Viaduct is 1,125 feet tall — that's 75 feet taller than the Eiffel Tower.

THE BRIDGE THAT ISN'T THERE

The Millau Viaduct can pull a pretty impressive disappearing act. Read this descriptive account to find out more.

Imagine the excitement in the town of Millau, France, on December 14, 2004. It was the opening of the Millau Viaduct. With this, the town could lay claim to having the tallest bridge in the world. In its first year, this amazing structure carried 4,430,000 cars — even more than was predicted.

But it isn't only the height of the bridge that sets it apart from other bridges. This bridge has the magical quality of almost disappearing against the horizon. And that's pretty impressive when the bridge deck alone weighs nearly 40,000 tons. The bridge has been described as "floating" above the river and having the "delicacy of a butterfly." Norman Foster, the architect, designed it to look as transparent as possible. He even used fewer and lighter materials to achieve this effect.

When she first saw the bridge, Caroline Wyatt, a Paris correspondent for the British Broadcasting Corporation, described it this way: "Seven slender piers support the roadway, rising into seven graceful pylons bound to the bridge with what look like cobwebs of steel."

At night the viaduct is lit. Even then it does not intrude on the landscape. It looks like a "ribbon of light" across the valley.

Take Note

This bridge was designed to disappear, to blend into the landscape. This unusual quality, along with its height record, makes the Millau Viaduct the most amazing bridge in the world.
- How does Norman Foster's different approach to bridge building influence the way you think about bridges and what makes them truly amazing?

We Thought …

Here are the criteria we used in ranking the 10 most amazing bridges.

The bridge:
- Featured amazing engineering
- Was challenging to build
- Is an impressive size in length and height
- Was artistically designed
- Has unique features
- Is of cultural/economic/historical importance
- Taught lessons in safety
- Had the ability to withstand natural disasters
- Was able to last for many years

	Rainbow	Monet	Kawarau	Quebec	Cendere	Lupu	Golden Gate	London	Akashi Kaikyo	Millau
Longest Span	276 ft	-	300 ft	1,800 ft	112 ft	1,804 ft	4,200 ft	various	6,532 ft	1,125 ft
Height	394 ft	-	143 ft	341 ft	-	164 ft	227 ft	various	213 ft	886 ft
Materials	sandstone	wood	schist stone, ironwood	66,600 tons of steel	92 ten-ton stones	50,700 tons of steel	83,000 tons of steel	various: wood, clay, stone, granite, concrete	200,000 tons of steel	Concrete and steel

What Do You Think?

1. Do you agree with our ranking? If you don't, try ranking them yourself. Justify your ranking with data from your own research and reasoning. You may refer to our criteria, or you may want to draw up your own list of criteria.

2. Here are three other bridges that we considered but in the end did not include in our top 10 list: Confederation Bridge, in Canada; Ponte Vecchio, in Italy; and Bridge on the River Kwai, in Thailand.
   - Find out more about them. Do you think they should have made our list? Give reasons for your response.
   - Are there other amazing bridges that you think should have made our list? Explain your choices.

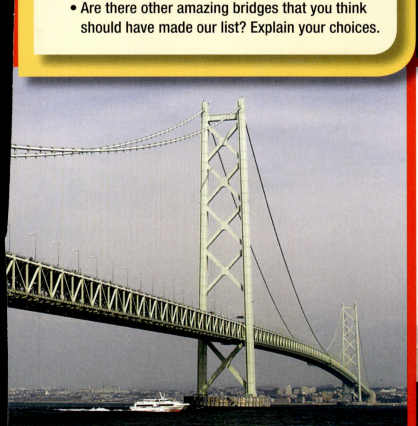

Index

A
Abutments, 25
Akashi Kaikyo Bridge, 38–41, 46
Arch bridge, 6–7, 16, 23–25, 27–29
Architect, 43–45
Arizona, 34–36
Asia, 24
Awaji, 39–40

B
Barcelona, 44
Batchelar, Warren, 16, 24, 28, 33, 37
Bungee jumping, 15–17

C
Cable-stayed bridge, 43
California, 27, 31, 41
Canada, 19, 47
Cantilever bridge, 19–20, 35
Caughnawaga Reservation, 21
Cement, 24
Cendere Bridge, 22–25, 29, 46
Central Otago, 15
China, 9, 27–28
Clay, 35–36, 46
Concrete, 4, 32, 35–36, 44, 46
Construction, 4, 13, 16, 19, 21, 25, 28, 32–33, 39, 44
Cooper, Theodore, 19–21

D
De Colechurch, Peter, 35–36
Dead weight, 20
Destruction, 8

E
Earth, 17, 37–38
Earthquake, 9, 21, 28, 31, 39–41
Eiffel Tower, 29, 44
Elastic potential energy, 17
Empire State Building, 29
Engineering, 4, 9, 12–14, 16, 19–21, 24–25, 27–29, 31–33, 36–37, 39–40, 43–44, 46
England, 35–37
Europe, 24
Expo 2010, 27

F
Foster, Norman, 43–45
France, 11, 17, 43–45

G
Garden, 10–12
Gatehouses, 35
Gephyrophobia, 27
Giverny, 11–13
Gold miners, 15
Golden Gate Bridge, 30–33, 46
Gorge, 7, 15–16, 28, 44
Granite, 35–36, 46
Gravitational potential energy, 17
Great Depression, 33
Guatemala, 41

H
Honshu, 39–40
Horizon, 43, 45
Huangpu River, 27–28
Human toll, 20
Hydraulic jacks, 44

I
Ice floes, 21
Iraq, 24

J
Japan, 11–13, 39–41

K
Kachina, 9
Kahta River, 23–24
Kawarau Bridge, 14–17, 46
Keystone, 25
Kinetic energy, 17
Kolob Arch, 9

L
Lake Powell, 8
Landscape Arch, 9
Le Bassin aux Nymphéas, 11
London, 34–37
London Bridge, 34–37, 41, 46
Lupu Bridge, 26–29, 46
Luwan, 26–27

M
Marin County, 32
Millau, 42–43, 45
Millau Viaduct, 42–46
Monet, Claude, 10–13
Monument, 7, 9
Mount Vesuvius, 24

N
Native Americans, 7
Natural bridges, 9
Navajo Mountain, 8
New River Gorge Bridge, 28
New York City, 29
New Zealand, 15–17
Nonnezoshe, 8
Nursery rhyme, 37

O
Owachomu, 9

P
Pacific Ocean, 32
Paris, 12, 29, 44, 45
Pedestrians, 20, 33
Pleistocene climate, 9
Poison, 12
Pozzolana, 24
Pudong, 26–27

Q
Quebec Bridge, 18–21, 46
Queenstown, 15–16

R
Railings, 11–12
Rainbow Bridge, 6–9, 13, 46
Rennie, John, 35–36
Richter scale, 28, 39–41
River Thames, 35–36

S
Sacred, 7–8
San Francisco, 31–33, 41
Sandstone, 7–8, 46
Scotland, 20
Septimius Severus, 23–25
Severan Bridge, 23
Shanghai, 27–29
Sheppard, B., 12
Shikoku, 40
Sipapu, 9
Slaves, 24
Soldiers, 24, 35
Spain, 44
Sproul, David Kent, 9
Steel, 16, 19–21, 27–28, 39–40, 44–46
St. Lawrence River, 19–21
Strauss, Joseph, 32
Suspension bridge, 4, 15, 30–31, 39–40, 43

T
Taft, William Howard, 7
Taiwan, 41
Tarkov, John, 21
Thatch, 35, 37
Tornadoes, 28
Transparent, 43, 45
Truss, 39
Tunnels, 16
Turkey, 23–24
Tushuk Tash, 9
Typhoon, 39, 41

U
United States, 7, 35, 41
Utah, 7–9

V
Virlogeux, Michel, 43
Virola, Juhani, 40
Voussoirs, 25

W
Water, 8, 11–12, 16, 20–21, 24, 28, 32, 36, 39
Weather, 8, 31–32, 39
West Virginia, 28
World War II, 8, 12
Wooden bridge, 11

Y
Yao Ming, 28–29